# Mary and Inner Healing:
# An Armchair Pilgrimage to Lourdes

# Mary
## and
# Inner Healing

*An Armchair Pilgrimage
to Lourdes*

GLORIA HUTCHINSON

*Nihil Obstat:*
> Rev. Hilarion Kistner, O.F.M.
> Rev. John J. Jennings

*Imprimi Potest:*
> Rev. Andrew Fox, O.F.M.
> Provincial

*Imprimatur:*
> +Daniel E. Pilarczyk, V.G.
> Archdiocese of Cincinnati
> May 9, 1980

The *Nihil Obstat* and *Imprimatur* are a declaration that a book or pamphlet is considered to be free from doctrinal or moral error. It is not implied that those who have granted the *Nihil Obstat* and *Imprimatur* agree with the contents, opinions or statements expressed.

Cover, book design and illustrations by Julie Van Leeuwen.

Photograph on back cover by David Hutchinson.

SBN 0-912228-76-8

*To Mary:*
*mother, sister, woman-friend*

# PREFACE

When the editor of our diocesan newspaper asked me to represent the publication on a pilgrimage to Lourdes, I laughed. He was offended. I assured him that I was pleased at the thought of flying off to the famous shrine in the French Pyrenees, but amused at the irony of the offer. This opportunity would have been highly prized by someone with a lifelong devotion to Our Lady. Instead it was being given to someone who had been juggling questions about Mary for years and hadn't quite decided what to do about her.

Like many Catholics, I no longer knew how to

relate to Mary. Certain that I had outgrown the childhood ways of novenas, May crownings and the public sing-song recitation of the rosary, I was uncertain about what should replace these traditions. Sometimes, while driving long distances alone on the Maine turnpike, lulled by the passing green of pastures and woods, I'd finger my rosary and think about Mary at Nazareth or Jerusalem. The prayers, slowly said, flowed like a subtle undercurrent to the heart's meditation. At times like these I would come close to recognizing Mary again, seeing her as mother, sister, woman-friend. But for the most part, she was absent from me.

A few months before the Lourdes trip, I read a commentary on the Wedding at Cana in Edward Leen's *In the Likeness of Christ.* I remember wondering why the significance of Mary's role in this Gospel story had never broken through to me before.

What moves Jesus to change the water into wine?

Although he knows the wine is gone and his hosts are about to be humiliated, he does nothing. Then his mother turns to him and says, "They have no more wine." His response—"Woman, how does this concern of yours involve me? My hour has not yet come"—seems to deny Mary's right to intervene. But in fact, it calls forth in her a new awareness. Jesus lets his mother know that the empty wine jars are insufficient to move him. His expression suggests that he will comply—if her request is based on other grounds.

And what are these other grounds?

Mary understands instantly. Jesus will respond

not because of the temporal need but because of her own intervention. He will act because she asks him to do so. He has commissioned her as intercessor. Fully accepting this new role, Mary instructs the servants: "Do whatever he tells you" (see John 2:1-11).

From Cana on, Mary speaks our need with powerful persuasion. Jesus makes that clear. On Calvary, he makes it final and universal, commending us with John into her care. If we accept her unique role, how should she affect our lives?

Lourdes gave me an answer. Despite my doubts about miraculous cures, my skepticism about apparitions, my fears about drowning in a sea of sentiment, Lourdes gave me an answer. *Par Marie a Jesus.* Through Mary to Jesus. Through Jesus to each other. It was simple. And overpowering. No pilgrim leaves the shrine untouched by this reality.

Of the 183 Americans on the Boston-National Pilgrimage to Lourdes in April, 1979, not one was miraculously cured. Among us were handicapped children, adults suffering from advanced kidney ailments, cancer and multiple sclerosis, persons paralyzed by accident or illness. One young man died within a month of our return from France.

Every pilgrim in our group, however, felt that he or she had been healed in some way. Each of us came home realizing how universal yet personal was the need for healing from sickness and sin in all its guises. Our old concept of healing—as a haven from affliction—was cast off as we clothed ourselves in a new understanding of how suffering is integrated into our lives as Christians.

Mary, who hallowed Lourdes by her presence in 18 apparitions to Bernadette Soubirous in 1858, continues to make her presence felt by millions of pilgrims each year. They speak to her in silence and song, in prayer and weeping. She speaks to them in imperceptible but undeniable ways, drawing them to Christ in the Eucharist and Christ in the other, healing their wounds and filling their emptiness.

This book is an attempt to share with those who may never go to Lourdes the rewards of my own pilgrimage. I hope it may make Mary more accessible to people who are seeking a new relationship with her.

I am grateful to Henry Gosselin, editor of *Church World,* Maine's Catholic weekly, and to Father Donald Gagne, S.M., director of the Lourdes Center in Boston, for making my pilgrimage possible. I appreciate the generous assistance of Barbara Yuodsnukis, who read and responded to the manuscript. And I am most thankful to my husband David, as well as our son David, for allowing me the quiet, uninterrupted time to write of Mary.

# CONTENTS

# INTRODUCTION

This is not a book to be read. It must be prayed. You are invited to become a pilgrim seeking Jesus through Mary.

Each day for eight consecutive days you are asked to give at least 30 minutes to a journey in faith—even if you never leave your armchair. Plan to embark on your daily pilgrimage from a place conducive to prayer; that is, a quiet room, a sun porch, a natural setting away from distractions.

From the first to the last day, you will follow a familiar path. First, a structured Meditation calls you aside to a prayerful environment, calling on your imagination to create some aspects of the physical surroundings of Lourdes. Small repeated designs mark the pauses on your walk, a few moments of quiet listening or reflection.

If you are making the pilgrimage with others, ask one person to read the Meditation section aloud, pausing after each paragraph and allowing several minutes of silence at each stop along the way.

If you are a solitary pilgrim, close your eyes at the end of each paragraph to "see" your surroundings. At each stop, lay the book down for a few minutes. Another approach is to record—or ask a friend to record—the Meditations and the accompanying Reflections; then let the tape recording be your guide.

In any case, this initial phase of the journey requires generosity with time and openness to the Spirit.

Next comes a Reflection that is an extension and a deepening of the Meditation. It focuses on Mary and on your relationship to her. Here is the heart of each day's pilgrimage: time to be with Mary, to hear her voice, to feel her touch. Like the Meditation, the Reflection calls for moments of extended silence, of being still before the Lord.

After the Reflection, you will return to the place of departure to consider how Mary has intervened in the life of a fellow pilgrim. The people you will meet in the Profile sections are real. They were members of the 1979 Boston-National Pilgrimage to Lourdes. They have consented to share their faith experience.

Each day's journey ends with a Prayer and an active Response. You are encouraged to replace or supplement these two stages according to your own wisdom. A Celebration for Pilgrims follows the eighth day.

One final word of advice: patience. Neither the meditations nor their outcome can be hurried. A teenage pilgrim named Eddie B., paralyzed by a bone, muscle and joint affliction, was asked on the eighth day of his pilgrimage, "Do you still have hope?" He responded with a knowing smile. "Hey, of course," he said. "A miracle takes a while."

# FIRST DAY:

# Turning
# to Mary

*Meditation*

Although Mary is always
and everywhere available to us, we seek her more
profitably in those places which, in a natural way,
reflect the qualities of her person. She chose to
appear to Bernadette Soubirous in the French village
of Lourdes, a little-known farming village set in the
foothills of the white-mantled Pyrenees Mountains.
Pilgrims to Lourdes are stunned by these mountains
which evoke memories of Isaiah's prophecy:

> *How beautiful upon the mountains
> are the feet of him who brings glad tidings,*

*Announcing peace, bearing good news,*
*announcing salvation, and saying to Zion,*
*"Your God is King!"*
(Isaiah 52:7)

Down from the high Pyrenees winds the Gave River. It flows through green fields where woolly sheep graze and wends its way past the stark grotto where Bernadette encountered the Mother of Jesus.

Because Mary has shown her preference for such a place, leave your present surroundings and let your imagination take you to a quiet place by the water. She has called you aside from work and worry, pain and discouragement, distraction and confusion. She is waiting for you. Perhaps she will be standing by a mountain stream or a hidden spring.

Take the narrow path to the place where you expect to find her. Hear the water music. Listen for the underlying theme. It may be rolling and sonorous. Or lighthearted, with a staccato splashing. Focus on the sound of the water for several minutes. Let it fill your ears. Let the water speak to you of peace.

The air is clean as though purified by the water. In it, you can detect the humble scents of grass, ferns and mosses. The water, too, has its own odor of

innocence, of life constantly renewed. Make the
words of the psalmist your own:

> *Beside restful waters he leads me;*
> *he refreshes my soul.*
>                    *(Psalm 23:2-3)*

Sit by the water and look into it. Let your eyes see
nothing else. Follow the flow and observe whatever
patterns are created. Notice the bubbles and swirls,
the white foam, the whirling eddies. Be soothed by
the beauty of the water.

Find a little pool where the water is untroubled.
Examine your reflection in it. Recognize that you
are a person who needs to be healed. Name the
affliction (physical, mental, emotional, spiritual)
that you perceive as an obstacle to wholeness. Let
the pleasing sound and sight of the water wash over
you. Accept the image in the pool, realizing that
each of us is handicapped in some way.

Continue to study your image for several minutes.
Do not allow resentment or bitterness to cloud the
water. Allow yourself to feel hopeful about the
resolution of your handicap.

# *Reflection*

Become aware now that you are not alone. In response to your effort to seek her, Mary is making herself present to you. Picture her standing at a short distance from you as she once stood on the banks of the Gave. She is beautiful and serene. Bernadette said of her, "She was bathed in light and alive . . . . She did nothing else but smile . . . . I would gladly die to see her again."

Mary is smiling at you. Whatever your age, she sees in you a beloved son or daughter, someone she has been hoping to hear from. Enjoy the gentle gladness her nearness creates in you.

Recognize in her the Mother you have always wanted, the one you cry out to in the darkness when you are in pain or fear, the one who can console you when no one else knows what is required. In her presence, here by this flowing water, be peaceful and confident. Let Mary bring out the best that is in you. Know that the Lord is with her.

Speak to Mary of your need for healing. Listen in silence as she speaks to you.

Now slowly leave this meeting place, knowing that you can return tomorrow. Take the memory of Mary with you as the sound of the stream becomes distant. Decide now to spend time every day fostering this relationship with Mary who will lead you to her Son. Begin to forge a firm expectation that she will always respond to you.

In gratitude for Mary's friendship, pray the Hail Mary.

# *Profile*

Y̶ou are not alone on your pilgrimage. As you come closer to Mary, you will see your fellow pilgrims more clearly. She wants you to know them, to realize that each is related to you. Consider your brother in Christ, Joe Z. Like you, he is handicapped and wants to be healed.

Joe bears his handicap visibly in his body. He is 20 and has been confined to a wheelchair by cerebral palsy since childhood. Unable to exert muscular control, Joe is dependent on others for help with ordinary tasks like eating, dressing, washing. His energies are shackled by a body that refuses to do his bidding. He yearns for a life of his own, a wife, a job, a future. Depression often provokes him to "take it out on" his family and friends, the able-bodied ones.

When Joe went to Lourdes, he wanted to "get closer to the Lord," to gain confidence in himself, to know that his suffering was not meaningless. He had no devotion to Mary. But he believed in the cures attributed to her intercession. He believed in the possibility that she would show herself a Mother to him.

During his eight-day pilgrimage, Joe began to reflect the signs of Mary's intervention. He began to recognize that his very affliction identified him more intimately with Jesus whose suffering "marred . . . his look beyond that of man" (Isaiah 52:14), but did not crush him under its weight. Joe realized that cerebral palsy enabled him to be a more Christ-like person, one who better understands others who suffer physical infirmity.

As he observed the wheelchair pilgrims around him, Joe recognized that many were more seriously handicapped than he was. He became mindful of their needs and their dark moods. With jokes and teasing, he urged them back to good humor. He felt a new responsibility to console others rather than waiting for someone to commiserate with him.

Joe shared his spiritual insights in a poem which he composed and asked a friend to put on paper. Entitled "The Good of Lourdes," it concludes:

> *It makes you sad that it has to end.*
> *But you will always remember the people you help.*
> *The good will always go with you.*

Joe's physical handicap remained exactly as it had been before he went to Lourdes. Only his perception of it changed. Mary lifted him out of depression. She showed him how to enter into the fellowship of pain with others, thus freeing him from the isolation imposed by self-pity. She offered him an opportunity to grow, to move onward in his pilgrimage.

"Before I came to Lourdes," Joe said, "I wished with all my heart that there might be a possibility of a cure. Now I know there's a reason why I'm this way. I'm just praying that I'll be able to cope with it."

## *Prayer*

Identifying yourself with Joe and with all your fellow pilgrims, turn to Mary in prayer:

> *Mary, help me to believe that you are my Mother,*
> *that Jesus intended you for me*
> *at Cana and at Calvary.*
>
> *Let me place my need to be healed*
> *in your hands,*
> *confident that your loving Son*
> *will hear*
> *your request.*
>
> *Lead me to the Christ who gives water*
> *from the well of life*
> *to all who thirst. Amen.*
>
> *Lord, be near me.*

## *Response*

Take a risk that sets aside any fear, pride or insecurity that prevents you from trusting a person who can be helpful to you in your healing process.

Do something today for a person whose burden is greater than your own. If possible, use humor as a healing touch.

Read and reflect on Luke 11:5-13, Two Parables on Prayer. Does your understanding and practice of prayer follow the advice given here by Jesus? If not, why not? What will you do to realize the truth of these parables in your life?

# Feeling
# Mary's Presence

*Meditation*

I t is time to continue now on your pilgrimage. Take nothing with you. Allow yourself to be childlike, unfettered by self-doubt and eager to embrace whatever experience the Lord has in store for you. Has he not told you, "Trust me when I tell you that whoever does not accept the kingdom of God as a child will not enter into it" (Luke 18:17)?

With the help of your imagination, take the path to the place where you encountered Mary yesterday. The water is again singing in a voice that pleases and soothes. Listen to its melody for a while. There is no need to hurry on.

Somewhere above the stream is a cavern. Approach this cave sculpted by wind and water. Observe the pattern of its formation, the ridges and clefts, the crannies and fissures. Notice that the rock, which at first appeared to be of one color, has several strata of varying hues. Layers of gray and sandy beige merge into slate and black as you look into the cavern's recesses.

Let your hand explore the stone surface. Is it smooth and cool to your touch? Rough and gravelled? What image does the rock suggest to you? Let the rock speak to you of permanence, of patience and reliability. There is a harsh beauty in the cavern, the beauty of simplicity that requires no adornment.

Sit down by the entrance to the cave. Savor the sense of timelessness it provides. Here you are not buffeted by change or transitory concerns.

Feel the solitude that insulates you from distractions. This solitude is as essential to you as a good meal or a good night's sleep. It sinks into your body, into your bones, into the core of your being where God dwells. Recall the words of the psalmist:

> *You will set me high upon a rock; you will give*
> *me rest;*
> *for you are my refuge.*
> *(Psalm 61:3-4)*

Continue to sit quietly for several minutes, allowing solitude to do its gentle work. Be as simple and silent as the stone.

When you feel rested, call to mind your image in the pool. Renew your expectation that the illness, affliction or problem that limits you can be surrendered to Mary's healing influence.

# *Reflection*

The person you have come to meet is here now. Picture her standing slightly inside the cavern with her bare feet on the cool rock. When Mary appeared to Bernadette, she chose this rough grotto carved out of a cliff above the Gave. Then, as now, the water murmured with pleasure at her presence.

Mary's smile welcomes you. Feel the confidence Jesus must have felt when that smile focused on him throughout his hidden years at Nazareth. Just as she embraced him in the Temple after three days of searching, so she now wants to embrace you because you too are her child. As she stood by him at Calvary, so will she remain with you when suffering threatens to extinguish faith. Having mothered Jesus in the flesh, she desires to mother him spiritually in you.

In silence, behold your Mother.

Listen attentively. Bernadette clearly heard the Lady speak. "Only it seems to me the sound of her voice reaches me here," she said, placing her hand over her heart.

Mary wants to speak to you in the same way. At Lourdes she spoke of prayer and penance and of the pleasure she took in Bernadette's visits. In the stillness of your heart, await whatever Mary has to say to you. If at first you cannot discern her voice, be content and patient like a child who knows that his mother will not ignore his requests. As you wait, quietly absorb the wordless compassion Mary offers you.

When your encounter is over, slowly leave the cavern. Be aware of Mary's personal love for you. Feel it like a warm mantle on your shoulders. As you return home, reflect on the ways in which your relationship with Mary may be changing. Are you willing to make a place for her in your life? Do you recognize your need for her as Mother and friend? Resolve that your pilgrimage will provide the answers.

In gratitude, pray the Hail Mary.

# *Profile*

No pilgrim ever went to Lourdes and returned home uncaring about the pain endured by others. In recognizing Mary as our mother, we come to recognize her Son in the physically handicapped, the sick, the aged and the sorrowing. In some, like Doris B., 33, and her five-year-old daughter Julie, we discern how Mary's influence can work in our lives if we are open to it.

When Doris discovered that her only daughter had neuroblastoma, an incurable cancer of young children, her one hope was Our Lady of Lourdes. "I was born on the Feast of the Immaculate Conception," she says, "and my own mother died when I was 11. So I've felt close to Mary for a long time." She decided to turn to Mary, mother to Mother, and ask for a gift that only Jesus could give: Julie's life.

The doctors who were treating Julie with radiation and chemotherapy predicted that she would not survive for more than a year or two. Doris wrestled with depression whenever she faced the probability of Julie's death. She wept when she considered the toll exacted by cancer and its treatment. Julie's curls were gone. Her bones were everywhere evident as though her body had forsaken all modesty in covering itself. Nausea often robbed her of appetite. Watching her daughter's decline, Doris countered with an act of faith that said: "If God wants Julie to be healed, she will be."

They went to Lourdes, hoping for a miracle. Doris did not expect a sudden blooming of the health Julie had once known. She did expect that somehow, through Mary's intercession, Julie would prevail. At the Grotto, Doris was overcome by the presence of a Mother whose love filled her with peace. She could think of nothing else. Fear and worry left her. "I took photographs all over Lourdes," she says, "but never at the Grotto. There my mind was totally on Mary."

Doris and Julie lit the tall white tapers that pilgrims use to remind Mary of their petitions — an unspoken tug at a Mother's sleeve, a silent *please*. They came home, feeling renewed and better able to cope with the difficulties of Julie's monthly chemotherapy.

The faith that enables Doris to believe in her daughter's future has been tried by the occasional setbacks Julie suffers. At times the elfin five-year-old seems too fragile to survive, a slender reed to be borne away on the wind. But each new day is part of the gift. And Julie is in her Mother's hands.

# *Prayer*

Identifying yourself with
Julie and Doris, and all your fellow pilgrims, turn to
Mary in prayer:

*Mother, teach me to trust,*
*to hope, to wait*
*for a healing which I*
*cannot prescribe.*

*Let my prayer be*
*open-handed,*
*that I may not grasp*
*at preconceived responses.*

*Remind me*
*that I am called*
*to heal the handicapped,*
*the sick, the sorrowing,*
*all who cry for Jesus' touch. Amen.*

*Lord, heal us.*

## Response

Think about the possible meanings of "accepting the kingdom of God as a child." Is your response to Jesus *childlike* in the Gospel sense (spontaneous, direct, generous, wholehearted)? How do your feelings about being healed reflect these positive characteristics? Decide to take at least one step toward becoming childlike in the way Jesus advised.

Look for an opportunity to turn an occasion of self-pity into a small triumph of unselfishness.

Comfort someone who is worrying about the health of another.

# Recognizing Mary's Power

*Meditation*

 Mary calls you to the
third day of your pilgrimage, your journey to meet
her. This is a journey taken daily by Christians
throughout the world. Be grateful if the pilgrimage
requires effort, concentration, the putting aside of
more pressing matters. At Lourdes Mary reminded
us of our need for penance, for denial of the
selfishness that darkens our vision.

Imagine it is evening, that quiet subdued time when
day and darkness co-exist. Take a white candle with
you and set out along the path toward the grotto

where you encountered Mary yesterday. Notice the agreeable weather. The air is warm. The wind has been hushed like a restless child. As the sun sets, its waning radiance is reflected in the stream. As you look up to the cavern, observe how evening softens the face of the rock with a veil of shadows.

Rest again by the cavern's mouth. Allow the prayerfulness of this place to flow into you. Let go of any pain, worry, stress or other negative feeling that may be holding you back. Relax, with your back against the stone. Breathe deeply, emptying out stored tension. Enjoy the muted fragrance of the evening.

The stream sighs as though remembering a lost love. Feel a sigh rising in you as you recall the Lady in the cavern — her beauty, her serenity, her smile. Hear Bernadette describe her first encounter with Mary:

> *I heard a distant murmur like a gust of wind. I looked up at the grotto. I saw a Lady dressed in white. She was wearing a white dress with a blue sash and had a yellow rose on each foot, the same color as the chain of her rosary.*

Dwell on this image of your Mother for several minutes until you know it well. Let the image arouse your confidence in Mary, your expectation of healing through her mediation.

# Reflection

L ight your candle and
stand facing the cavern. There, a few feet beyond
the circle of copper light created by the flame,
picture Mary in white and blue. Greet her with
biblical praise:

> *Hail, Mary, full of grace,*
> *the Lord is with you.*
> *Blessed are you among women,*
> *and blessed is the fruit of your womb, Jesus.*

Hold your candle aloft so that its glow clarifies her
expression. Her eyes reveal the pleasure your
greeting has given her. She holds you in her gaze, a
Mother searching her child's soul. Her loving
acceptance of you is as clear as if she had taken your
hand or kissed your cheek.

There is no need to say anything. Mary sees where
your need for healing lies. She wants you to remain
with her until the candle dies down. Look into her
face and recognize the authority given to her by
Christ at Cana. Hers is the power of limitless love.
God who is mighty has done great things for her.
And she can do great things for you. Through her
intercession, Christ has healed the sick and
reconciled the sinner.

Listen now for Mary's voice.

Be open now to healing — both to the healing of suffering (physical, mental, emotional, spiritual) and to the deeper healing of fear and unwillingness to suffer. Recall that when you are weak, you are strong. Let God work his will in you because that is the path to your greatest happiness. Repeat with Mary:

*"Let it be done to me as you say."*
*(Luke 1:38)*

Your candle is burning low. Take your leave of Mary and return to the path. You have much to think about. As the candle lights your way home, so will Mary guide you in the ways of the Lord. She will open your eyes to his presence in others — others whose pain and need you might never have noticed had you kept walking in your own way. Be thankful that she has invited you to be a pilgrim. Pray the Hail Mary.

# *Profile*

Open your heart to your fellow pilgrims, those who walk with you in faith. Each bears his or her particular suffering, as personal as a name. Although we can not fully understand the suffering of another, we can enter into it by listening, caring, touching. We can reaffirm the hope that keeps all of us on the path, that refuses to let even one fall by the wayside without notice.

Consider Debbie M., a beautiful dark-haired young woman of 17. When she was 14, Debbie had the lower half of her leg amputated because it was infected with bone cancer. An athletic and attractive teenager, she refused to be defeated by what could have been a devastating surgery.

"Everyone else was crying," she recalls, "But I loved all the attention, the flowers, the presents. I remember saying good-bye to my toes. I realized the doctor was going to take my leg, but they were going to give me another one and it didn't really seem that bad."

The amputation was only the first test of Debbie's spirit. Six months of chemotherapy followed; then another six months of deceptively good health. Debbie was elated. She served in student government, performed in the drama club, fell in love.

Then the monthly X-rays revealed a shadow on her lungs. Further exploration uncovered four tumors. "I threw my get-well cards on the floor and yelled and cried. My mom told me I could see my grandmother in heaven. I couldn't stand any of it. It was terrible," she says.

Debbie's mother urged her to join the Lourdes pilgrimage. At first she refused. "I have a thing about pride. It's hard for me to ask for help for myself. A miracle is something you can't get on your own. You realize you have to ask God for it. And for someone like me to believe enough to ask for a miracle — well, that's a miracle in itself," Debbie says.

Eventually she agreed to go to Lourdes despite misgivings about her lack of devotion to Mary and her concept of herself as "not a very religious person." Debbie took it for granted that Mary calls only the devout to her shrine. She had forgotten Jesus' admonition to the Pharisees who criticized him for socializing with tax collectors rather than aligning himself with the righteous. "People who are in good health do not need a doctor," Jesus told them, "sick people do" (Matthew 9:12).

Debbie's pilgrimage began with prayer as narrow as a rivulet on a mountainside. But each day it gathered force until it became as wide and confident as a river on its way to the sea. With every visit to the Grotto, Debbie felt herself shedding pride, fear and, finally, her desperate need for a physical cure. Mary touched her in such reassuring ways that Debbie experienced a profound joy.

Through the counseling of a Marist priest, the caring gestures of elderly Italian pilgrims who could not speak English, and the direct consolation she gives in prayer, Mary led Debbie to the point where she could say, "It's strange, but I don't even really care now. When I came here, I wanted my leg to grow back and the tumors to be gone. But the faith of everyone here is so overwhelming that it makes you forget about yourself. When I see people lying on stretchers, I feel that my suffering is insignificant. I want to push those who are in wheelchairs. Mary just makes it so easy for you to give of yourself."

After her return home, Debbie had further surgery for removal of a lung tumor. Then began a series of experimental chemotherapy treatments intended to halt the progress of cancer to other parts of her body. As the treatments continue, Debbie is sometimes depressed and frightened by the uncertainty of her own survival. Those are the times when she must, through meditative remembering, return to the Grotto for reassurance and the courage to embrace life.

# Prayer

Identifying yourself with Debbie, and all your fellow pilgrims, turn to Mary in prayer:

*Mary, you call us forth*
*from the darkness of unknowing*
*and affliction.*

*You call us into faith*
*and fruitful caring.*

*Lead us on,*
*never letting us forget*
*the hand*
*waiting to be taken,*
*the Jesus-face*
*longing to be seen. Amen.*

*Lord, help us.*

## Response

Do something today for a person whose handicap or illness seems to be incurable. Take either the direct approach (a visit, call or letter) or the indirect (petitional prayer, fasting for the person's intentions, offering your own suffering in cheerful patience for the alleviation of the other's pain). Act today. Don't be satisfied with a good intention packed away where moths can consume it.

Be alert for the positive ways in which people mother you. Let them see your gratitude for this kind of caring.

Read and reflect on Luke 2:41-52, The Finding of Jesus in the Temple. Let this Scripture reading serve as a prelude to an attentive praying of the fifth joyful mystery of the rosary. Consider the relationship between Mary and Jesus at this point in their lives. Imitate Mary who, when she does not grasp the meaning of Jesus' words, mulls them over in her heart.

# Honoring
# Mary

## *Meditation*

Before you embark today, take time to be glad about your unfolding friendship with Mary. Perhaps she means more to you now than she ever has, and you realize that you have hardly begun to know her. Perhaps you feel a delight that spills over into generous prayer: "May the heart of Mary be in each Christian to proclaim the greatness of the Lord; may her spirit be in everyone to exult in God" (St. Ambrose).

Imagine it is midmorning when the sun is gathering strength for its noonday climb. Leave your usual surroundings and follow the same path, but when you get to the stream cross over it and find on the other side a wide clearing. Before you is a field lush with waving grasses and wild flowers. Walk slowly into the field, feeling the grass against your legs and the soft, matted earth under your feet. Hear the swishing and humming sounds that give fields an air of quiet activity. Feel the mild breeze and the sense of liveliness that emanates from every created thing around you.

Find a knoll or a ledge, a place from which you can survey the field. Rest there, drawing nourishment from nature's plenty. Observe the particular beauty of each flower your gaze falls on: the daisy with its dark eye trained above, its petals spreading outward like rays of the sun; the buttercup, its face shining like that of a saint; the purple clover with its trinitarian leaves and easygoing grace. Nodding and bowing in the breeze, the wild flowers speak to you of God's lavish love. Their fragrances blend in an incense that rises before his face. They praise him by fulfilling his idea of them.

Be at ease here among these flowers where God's glory is as perceptible to you as the midday sun. Like the daisy, lift your face to your Father and praise him with your being. Let no words come between you. In silence, feel his love for you, exactly as you are.

*"I have called you by name: you are mine."*
*(Isaiah 43:1)*

In the clear light of your Father's love, look at the affliction or illness you have identified as your handicap. Accept it as one aspect of your being at this time in your life, an aspect that may give him as much glory as whatever qualities you consider most desirable in yourself. Accept the possibility that your handicap may be, in the Father's image of you, something beautiful and even necessary to your process of becoming. Let go and say *yes* to the Father's vision of you.

## *Reflection*

**E**njoy the sense of peace your *yes* brings. Feel your closeness to Mary and take her words as your own: "Let it be done to me as you say" (Luke 1:38).

As a sign of her unity with you, she is standing in the field, waiting to share your happiness. She is clothed with the sun and crowned with 12 stars, a woman of great beauty and magnetism. Her being praises God because she has perfectly fulfilled his will. She is both Queen of Heaven and humble servant of Yahweh. But you recognize something more in her and call her Mother.

Gather a bouquet of wild flowers to honor her in the pilgrim's traditional gesture. Be drawn to her as the one who is mothering your spiritual growth, guiding you on the way to wholeness, healing the divisions within you. Lay your lovely daisies at her feet. Be content to look at Mary. Listen for her voice.

You are totally at peace in your Mother's presence.

You can say with the psalmist:

> *I have stilled and quieted*
>   *my soul like a weaned child.*
> *Like a weaned child on its mother's lap,*
>   *[so is my soul within me.]*
>                   *(Psalm 131:2)*

Rest a while.

When you are ready, set out on the way home. Peace surrounds you as the sun surrounded Mary. Keep everything you have considered today in your heart. As you walk through the field and come upon the stream, hum a melody in harmony with it. Pray the Hail Mary.

# *Profile*

**J**ust as this pilgrimage may uncover hidden truths about your handicap, so did a Lourdes pilgrimage reveal to one man how his paralysis enabled him to enter into the discipleship of suffering.

Oscar C.'s story might well have been a tragedy. Between the ages of 48 and 50, he suffered three heart attacks and had major cardiac surgery. Although Oscar was overweight, he recovered rapidly and was, within a few months after surgery, walking six miles a day. When friends in Marriage Encounter asked Oscar and his wife Dolores to accompany them to the Shrine of St. Anne de Beaupre in Canada, they agreed. It seemed a perfect opportunity to give thanks for Oscar's recovery.

Shortly after the two couples crossed the Canadian border, Dolores suggested that they pray the Our Father together. Five minutes later the driver lost control and the car careened over a steep embankment. Oscar and his wife were thrown together in the back seat.

"I was totally immobile and had no pain" Oscar recalls. "I knew it had to be a spinal injury."

Despite the neurosurgeon's prediction that Oscar would never again move any part of his body, he eventually regained enough mobility in his right arm to operate an electric wheelchair. He spent three years moving in and out of hospitals.

Because his faith was still intact, Oscar was able

to help other handicapped patients by his example. They expected a man who had been reduced to complete physical dependency in midlife to be bitter and self-pitying. They were surprised to find him cheerful and concerned about other people.

During those three years, Oscar was annually invited to join the Lourdes pilgrimage. Each time he declined because of his apprehensions about the physical problems a long trip would entail. He was subject to pneumonia. He could not remain sitting for more than seven hours and he had difficulties with ostomy appliances.

Dolores had other fears. How could she deal with the labor of caring for Oscar on the plane and in Lourdes? What if they should be involved in an accident? "I never told Oscar," she says, "but I was afraid of not having any time to myself, afraid of everything."

In 1979 Oscar said yes to Lourdes, and Dolores agreed. A chance meeting with a nun who told him he was a courageous Christian witness in the manner of St. Paul convinced Oscar that he could no longer be deterred by fear of what might happen. "I decided that God must have a plan for me. I forgot all my problems. I put my hand in the Father's and let come what may," he remembers.

Mary's response to his decision was not long in coming. From the moment the plane lifted off, Oscar felt transfixed and elated. He had no trouble remaining seated for 12 hours. The usual pressure sores did not appear during the trip or at any time during or after his pilgrimage.

When a Marist priest gave a homily to the handicapped pilgrims, Oscar "hinged on every word and every pause." The message stunned him. He heard it as clearly as Saul heard the voice of Christ. "You who are handicapped are the chosen people. You have been blessed by God and he has made his will clear to you. From your wheelchair, you must reflect his love. There is no other way. Go forth and do the Father's work."

Oscar's response to the message was unconditional. "That was my miracle," he says. "I opened myself up more than ever to seek and help anyone who would let me. It didn't matter if people rejected me or laughed at me. Now I had the strength to carry on like an apostle, to tell others how I feel about my handicap, about the Father's love and what Mary has done for me."

As Oscar says, all his healing was done on the inside. His body remains inert. Greater endurance allows him regularly to visit hospital patients, handicapped young people, neighbors and friends. He and Dolores are facing the mutual difficulties of his dependence on her with deeper patience and tranquillity. Oscar has been reconciled with his younger brother after seven years of unforgiving bitterness.

Dolores still hopes for the miracle of her husband's mobility. But Oscar feels that his handicap fits him for his aspostolate. "My relationship with Our Lady has given me this outlook on life. When I am low, I think of my trip to Lourdes and of Mary and all those beautiful pilgrims around me. Then I feel very fortunate."

# *Prayer*

Identifying yourself with Oscar and Dolores, and all your fellow pilgrims, turn to Mary in prayer.

> *Dear Lady,*
> *we scatter flowers*
> *of thankfulness*
> *at your feet.*
>
> *We lift our hearts*
> *like wine-filled chalices*
> *to praise*
> *your beloved Son.*
>
> *Spirit-led,*
> *we sunder*
> *our porcelain self-images*
> *to liberate*
> *truth. Amen.*
>
> *Lord Jesus, be praised!*

# Response

If Mary is becoming an integral part of your life, share something from your pilgrimage experience with a friend.

Write a short litany of praise to Mary, selecting titles for her that have particular meaning to you. (For example: "Mother of Pilgrims, pray for us." "Our Lady of the Fields, guide us.")

Place a bouquet (fresh or handmade from tissue or construction paper) next to your Bible today as a reminder that Mary is leading you to Christ.

FIFTH DAY:

# Committing Oneself to Mary's Care

*Meditation*

P repare yourself for the fifth day of your pilgrimage, realizing how far you have come and how expectant you are about the distance yet to be traveled. As Mary's tenderness, her wisdom, her strength become more evident to you, your desire to be with her wells up naturally. You realize now how good it is to sit at the feet of our Mother most admirable, Mother most amiable, Mother of healing grace.

Today when your imagination brings you to the stream, walk along its mossy bank, heading neither

47

toward the cavern nor the field. Let the happy memories of these places accompany you as you continue. When you notice a narrow path leading into a stand of hardwood trees, turn off in this new direction. The path is hemmed in by maple saplings and young birches, their summer leaves brilliant green. Through the canopy of leaves, the sun draws dappled patterns on the path. Where shade predominates, the white-barked birches stand forth like tapers in a darkening room.

As the sound of the stream recedes and the path's origin disappears behind you, feel the seclusion of this wooded retreat. Hear the rustling of leaves like hushed voices in a great cathedral. Let your fingers run lightly through the overhanging leaves. Observe their distinctive textures and hues. Your eyes find rest in this sea of passing greenery.

Above you on a maple branch sits a plump brown sparrow. Concealed by the foliage, he is as secure as a friar in his cell. His appearance is humble and modest. But his song is flamboyant, suddenly parting the silence with apparent joy. Stop and listen. The sparrow sings from a full heart, aiming his bird-chant at the heart of his Creator. He sings as though he knows that not a single sparrow falls to the ground without the Father's consent (see Matthew 10:28-31), as though he realizes that his only concern is to give praise, and all the rest will be given to him.

Imitate the sparrow in his single-mindedness. Realize that the Creator of the universe, the Father of all, the *Abba* of Jesus desires to hear your song, the song of praise your life becomes when you trust entirely in him. Has he not promised that you are worth more than a flock of sparrows? Has he not vowed that every hair of your head has been counted and that there is nothing for you to fear?

Hear again the song of the sparrow, appreciating the sense of freedom and gratitude he projects. Is your song a reflection of your faith? Or has it been stifled by illness, anxiety and doubt? Let yourself feel the freedom of a child of God, a child who knows that everything he or she needs will be provided—and more besides. Believe that whatever healing you truly need will be forthcoming.

# *Reflection*

Your Mother waits on the path ahead of you. She is clothed in white and serenaded by many sparrows. Joy illumines her face at your coming. Repeat with her:

> *God who is mighty has done great things for me,*
> *    holy is his name.*
>
> (*Luke 1:49*)

Share Mary's faith in the Spirit who conceives Jesus in us, her faith in the Father who is ever mindful of us and whose promises last forever.

Sit quietly at Mary's feet and listen for her voice.

When you are ready, take leave of Mary and follow the path back to the stream. Hold the image of the sparrow in your mind, remembering the gospel message he embodies. Because you are a pilgrim, and pilgrims have always offered songs to Mary, sing your favorite hymn to her now as you walk along.

# *Profile*

Most of us recognize
ourselves as pilgrims only at those brief times we set
apart for spiritual journeying. It is the rare soul who
finds identity and fulfillment in being a pilgrim
fulltime. Jackie M. is a 27-year-old victim of
cerebral palsy. He gets around by pushing his
wheelchair backwards with his feet. His hands,
constrained perpetually to a clamped position, are of
little use. He cannot stand or sit straight; his chin
often drops onto his chest when the burden of his
head becomes too great. His speech is seriously
impaired.

A poem written by Jackie's cousin, Salesian
priest Father Kenneth McAlice, suggests both his
physical appearance and his spiritual awareness:

> *Jackie flays the air like angels wounded;*
> *His legs are strapped but writhe,*
> *Denying a 'natural' blessing.*
> *But Jackie is the only one*
> *Who ever hugged me.*
>
> *His syllables gush in garbled nonsense*
> *But scorn the lack of vocalism,*
> *Mouthing innocent poetry.*
> *For Jackie is the only one*
> *Who said I love you.*

When Jackie was 20, he went to Lourdes for the

first time. The Franciscan Missionaries of Mary, who staff the hospital where Jackie lived for 10 years, had taught him to pray the rosary and the Mass responses. At Our Lady's Grotto he prayed without inhibition, a sparrow unfettered by the fear that he might be out of tune.

Those who hear Jackie pray discover that devotion is no fragile and flowery thing that blooms only in agreeable climates. His prayer words are raucous yet recognizable because he labors to shape them into familiar forms. His voice is confined to the heavy tones of a bass drum. But his spirit soars beyond the range of the flute. Jackie's prayer expresses a vigorous praise that thrives in rocky soil and defies the cold winds of constant difficulty. Fellow pray-ers return to their own prayer with a deep gratitude.

At Lourdes Mary so captivated Jackie that he never wanted to leave. On the final day of his first pilgrimage he hid in the cafeteria, hoping that no one would find him. To the nurse who found his hideaway, he explained that Lourdes is his home. Jackie has been sent by a sponsor on the spring pilgrimage each year since then. His love for the Grotto, for prayer and for his fellow pilgrims is too powerful to be denied.

Mary has made a difference in Jackie's life. She has given him the insight to see how profoundly his example encourages people less handicapped than himself. Jackie realizes that by being a pilgrim he brings benefits to others through his prayers, his concern and his faith.

Every day at the custodial hospital which is his home, Jackie stations his wheelchair in the lobby so he can greet visitors with a pleasant, "How are you?" Then he makes the rounds of wards and rooms to visit patients and assure them of his prayers. His parents, Phyllis and John, say they are thankful for the unity and the example of faith Jackie has given their family.

Listening to the rosary on the radio, Jackie prays along and remembers the Lady of the Grotto. In April, at pilgrimage time, he sits expectantly on the edge of his wheelchair like a bird on a branch, poised to fly home.

# Prayer

Giving thanks for Jackie and all sick or handicapped persons who have transcended their suffering through faith and trust, turn to Mary in prayer:

*Mother of Jesus,*
*Mother of Mercy,*
*your love empowers us*
*to move beyond*
*dead-end suffering*
*and easy devotion.*

*Your love enables us*
*to sing our song*
*in and out of season.*

*Mother of Jesus,*
*Mother of Mercy,*
*mold my prayer for healing*
*into an open water jar*
*to receive the choice wine*
*of your Son's blessings. Amen.*

*Lord Jesus, fill me.*

# Response

Read aloud and reflect on the meaning of Psalm 84:

> *How lovely is your dwelling place,*
> *O L*ORD *of hosts!*
> *(Psalm 84:2)*

Are you like those whose hearts are set upon the pilgrimage? Do you trust the Lord God to withhold no good thing from you?

As an exercise in trust, make yourself dependent on someone for something you need or want. Be patient and do not allow yourself any expression of dissatisfaction or correction.

Today when you feel like complaining, think about Jackie.

# Committing Others to Mary's Care

*Meditation*

As friendship with Mary sinks its roots into our consciousness, we feel more intensely our relationship to one another. Because she is the Mother of Compassion, Mary schools us in suffering *with* the other. She shows us the pain under a mask of pleasantries, the sorrow hunched like a wounded rabbit behind a camouflage of words. She urges us to see ourselves in the faces where hardship has written its unsparing lessons. And she opens our hearts to the deep joy that underlies sorrow when we, Christ-like, willingly endure suffering because love demands it.

Prepare for today's journey by asking Mary to lead you to the Shrine where her pilgrims gather. On the way, discard the weight of distractions and troubles. Hear the stream rushing along, eager to reach its destination. Feel the blessing of the late afternoon sun on your back and shoulders. A light breeze ruffles the maple leaves. In the distance, sparrows are offering Vespers. Their song evokes in you a desire to praise.

Approach the cavern and pause there to rest against the rock. Let the memories of this silent place still any thoughts that now disturb you. Begin climbing the slope above the cavern. Breathe deeply, exhaling all your inner fatigue and inhaling the bracing air. Your spirit responds to the elevation, proclaiming with the psalmist:

> *I lift up my eyes toward the mountains;*
> *whence shall help come to me?*
> *My help is from the L*ORD.
> *who made heaven and earth.*
> *(Psalm 121:1-2)*

As the cliff levels off, there before you is a large, open area with smooth walkways converging on a central square. At the far end of the square is an altar draped in sun-drenched white. Behind the altar, above and to the right, is a statue of a crowned woman. The statue has admirable beauty and grace, but you realize that it is only an inadequate suggestion of the reality it represents. Hear around you the quiet sounds of other pilgrims making their way toward the altar. They share your anticipation and your conviction that the Woman is worth seeking.

Find a place where you can see the altar and watch the gathering crowd. Notice that there are pilgrims in wheelchairs, pilgrims on stretchers and crutches, pilgrims bent like wheat in the wind.

Look closely at the handicapped teenager whose arms and legs hang slack and useless. His mouth is agape. When he smiles, a twisted grimace creases his face in a parody of cheerfulness. His fingers are inert and stiffly separated, refusing to work together for the common good. The hat that has fallen down over his eyes symbolizes his inadequacy.

Look closely at the middle-aged mother whose vitality has been eroded by a cancer that grows within her like an evil offspring. Unable to care for her family, she has been stripped of the maternal responsibilities that gave her satisfaction and purpose. Weakness is a constant humiliation to her. In her face, you see the handiwork of helplessness.

Look closely at the aging nun, her red-rimmed eyes and lips outstanding in a waxen face, her veiled head sagging like an untended plant. Affliction has darkened her memories of joyful faith and productive service. The rosary wound around her arthritic hands binds her to the faith that suffers and abides.

Identify with your fellow pilgrims. Do not turn away or try to insulate yourself from their pain.

Enter into it. Feel the shame provoked by thoughtless pity: "Oh, you poor thing. I'm so sorry." Feel the stares that coldly turn persons into curiosities. Feel the rejection of those who are offended by the sight of the afflicted.

Be one with those who cry out for healing.

## Reflection

Turn now to the statue of the Woman. See past the marble to the warm reality of Mary, Mother of Mercy. Her arms are extended to embrace each person who has come to her for help. Her head is tilted forward in the attitude of one focused on listening. She is luminous with loving attention. Speak to her of your own needs and seek her intercession for all pilgrims. Listen for her voice.

Mary has called you here not for herself, but for her Son. The altar reminds you of his Eucharistic presence, of his desire to be with you in a relationship more intimate than the vine to the branches or the shepherd to his sheep. Within you he finds his dwelling place. Through you he touches others, giving them a glimpse of his perfect love. As the Father loves him, so he loves you. And he does not ask that you love others in the same way; he commands it.

The Mass is celebrated throughout the day and into the night at Lourdes because Mary arouses in pilgrims a hunger for the Bread of Life. She leads them to the altar where they offer themselves, with the Son, to the Father. The liturgy is then intensified by a powerful outpouring of pure devotion. United in their recognition of each other as brothers and sisters, the pilgrims experience Christ's presence in their midst with a clarity that consoles and inspires.

Gaze at the altar and remember Jesus in the Eucharist. Slowly repeat his sacred name, savoring its sweetness. Recall his promise:

> *The man who feeds on my flesh*
> *and drinks my blood*
> *remains in me, and I in him.*
>             *(John 6:56)*

Give yourself to him with abandon, realizing that he is your health, your happiness, your completion, your life.

When you have given yourself, trusting Jesus to sustain you in all things, look again on the faces of your fellow pilgrims, imprinting them on your memory. Commit each of them to Mary's care and resolve that you will minister to those whom affliction has made dependent and powerless. On the way home, pray the Hail Mary for the gift of compassion.

# *Profile*

In some people, illness builds a barrier. Behind that wall, the sick one gathers us his remaining energies, determined to spend them in pursuit of whatever satisfactions are yet available to him. He exempts himself from the requirements of charity, demanding that others pay him homage in sympathy and indulgence of his desires.

In others, illness opens the floodgates. The afflicted person determines to spend herself in service while she yet has strength to help another. She redoubles her practices of charity, realizing that:

> *One who has no love for the brother he has seen cannot love the God he has not seen.*
> *(1 John 4:20)*

Consider Mary K., a nursing supervisor in a custodial hospital for the multiply-handicapped. For over 20 years, she has cared for victims of mental retardation, cerebral palsy, stroke, severe respiratory and kidney diseases. Her solicitude has revived hope in patients tempted to despair. Now middle-aged, Mary is herself handicapped by multiple sclerosis.

When the illness was diagnosed a few years ago, Mary decided to go on nursing until her progressive symptoms made work impossible. "I've managed quite well, although I can't lift or push the patients in wheelchairs anymore. I have trouble walking and sometimes I overstep a stair because of difficulties with my vision. But there are still plenty of things I can do. Unless my presence gets to be a concern to others at the hospital, I'll stay on. That's where I belong," she says.

Each spring when she joins the Lourdes pilgrimage, Mary comes closer to making the complete transition from nurse-helper to handicapped patient. Her affliction has given her a greater empathy with those whose helpless bodies she once tended. She prays to Mary not for a cure, but for a more robust faith that will sustain her through the physical degeneration yet to come.

"Our Lady is always there, always touching people's lives. I ask her for the strength to cope with things and to keep me going as long as I can fulfill a need," Mary says. She seeks not to be healed, but to go on healing.

# Prayer

Identifying yourself with Mary K. in her desire to serve, turn to Mary in prayer:

> *Mary, be my school of compassion,*
> *my tutor of gentle caring.*
> *Release the healer in me*
> *that I may minister.*
> *Tell me your Jesus stories*
> *to show me the way.*
>
> *"When my Son sobbed over the faithlessness of Jerusalem, he cried out, 'How often have I wanted to gather your children together as a mother bird collects her young under her wings, and you refused me!' (Luke 13:34) Hear him, my Beloved, who mothers you and teaches you to go and do likewise."*
>
> *Speak, Lord,*
> *for your chick*
> *is listening. Amen.*

## *Response*

Be a mother to someone today by listening to his or her troubles, offering guidance if you are able to do so, recognizing and encouraging goodness in the person you have chosen.

Make a list of every person you know who is sick or handicapped in some way. Keep the list with your Bible or your rosary as a reminder that these people need to be supported in prayer every day.

Read and reflect on John 11:1-44, The Raising of Lazarus. In what ways is Jesus' deep compassion made evident to us? For what reasons does Jesus weep? Consider how you would have felt had you been standing outside the tomb with him. Realize that, through the Scripture, you are there with him.

# SEVENTH DAY:

# Through Mary
# to Jesus

## *Meditation*

Pilgrims to Lourdes are often surprised to learn that Bernadette Soubirous, who was an instrument of healing for others, never expected or received physical healing herself. Until her death at 35, she suffered from asthma and a painful tubercular knee. She bore all this with patience because she recognized sickness as a special bond with the suffering Christ. In her "white chapel"—a canopied bed in the convent infirmary—Bernadette prayed constantly, asserting, "I am happier on my bed with my crucifix than a queen on her throne."

With gratitude for the witness of St. Bernadette, leave your usual place and let your imagination take you down the path by the stream. The sky is overcast with the dullness of tarnished silver and the air is still. The stream is subdued to a thoughtful murmuring. Neither the foliage nor the sparrows offer any accompaniment as you walk along this familiar way. Nature is mute, as though contemplating a mystery beyond her province.

Take the path through the hardwoods where you encountered Mary. Today the trees are silent sentinels. Continue until you emerge into the open. A barren hillside rises before you. It is covered with a grassy stubble broken here and there by bare-faced rocks. There is nothing in this scene to draw you on but a towering wooden cross at the summit of the hill. Climb toward the cross, focusing your attention on its stark outline against the gray sky.

As you come closer, observe that the cross is rough-hewn from pine boards. It is heavy and without distinction. Touching it, realize that its rough surface and solid mass provide no consolation. Of itself, the cross is nothing but a dead thing, a reminder of the ancient gibbet on which criminals hung. But you see in it a Tree of Life, an emblem of hope, the signature of a loved one.

Kneel at a short distance from the cross. Hear the awesome promise of Jesus, when he knew his hour had come:

> *". . . and I—once I am lifted up from earth—*

*will draw all men to myself."*
*(John 12:32)*

Feel Christ drawing you now.

See the image of the Man of Sorrows. See him who realized perfectly that suffering would not pass away until he passed through it, who decisively and willingly accepted it out of unfathomable love. Recognize that by his crucifixion, Jesus conferred dignity and meaning on all human suffering which is surrendered to the Father's will. Behold the Man.

## Reflection

Realize that none of us stands before the cross alone. Mary is always there, ever faithful, ever mindful of our need to accept whatever form the cross takes in our own lives. She is our Mother of Sorrows, her face a magnificent portrait of compassion. Dwell on her face. Absorb her expression. She does not clutch sorrow like some dark possession brewing hatred, depression or revenge. Her sorrow is a selfless thing, a pure reflection of her Son's forgiving love.

Hear the voice of Jesus speaking to you: "Behold your Mother."

Let the healing power of his words penetrate you. Accept his gift, accept its consoling reality. Mary is not some heavenly being appointed to act as a mother toward you. She is wholly human and wholly your Mother. Through her, Jesus realizes the joy of mothering you, bringing you gradually and surely into the fullness of faith.

Be silent before Mary and hear her.

As Mary remained with Jesus in the hour of his death, so shall she remain with you. Recall her words to Bernadette: "I do not promise to make you happy in this world, but in the next." She does not promise miraculous cures—although she has delivered many. She does not promise dramatic conversions—although she has inspired many. She does not promise liberating forgiveness—although she has led many to reconciliation after years of separation and guilt. She is our Mediatrix, the means by which God's freeing grace comes to us.

Reaffirm your trust in Mary, your faith in her intercessory power. Believe that she is the channel by which healing will flow into your life. Rest in silent peace with this conviction.

When you are ready to leave, prostrate yourself before the cross as a sign of your identity with Jesus. The image of this rough cross will remain with you as a reminder that suffering cannot be denied or refused. It must be passed through before it can be integrated into your imitation of Christ.

As you return home, feel nature's silence as a comforting touch, a sign of communion. Feel the spiritual distance you have traveled today and be grateful for it.

Pray the Hail Mary, concentrating particularly on the second stanza.

# *Profile*

While many pilgrims receive physical healing, others face death while on pilgrimage. We cannot ignore this hard truth or gloss it over with sentiment: A person, who prays fervently for health and life, dies. The departure remains a mystery to us. Death appears as a cruel separation, a deaf ear turned to the pleas of the living. The prayer of Job does not enter easily into our hearts:

> *"The Lord gave and the Lord has taken away;*
> *blessed be the name of the Lord!"*
> *(Job 1:21)*

Consider your brother Rob L., an energetic young man until, at 17, he began to feel the progressively destructive effects of Hodgkin's disease. Three months of chemotherapy bought him a brief period when no new nodules appeared and the disease seemed to have subsided. Rob, his parents and his three brothers and sisters were elated. Their prayers had been answered. Fear about Rob's future was buried under layers of optimism and relief.

Within weeks, the nodules again erupted. Rob was required to undergo extensive and exhaustive chemotherapy. His mother Loretta recalls that he developed a terrible revulsion for the intraveneous needles that led to violent nausea. "We applied

Lourdes water to Rob's arms and the needles seemed less painful to him," Loretta says. Her son continued to go out with his friends, work at a supermarket, and live as normally as his deteriorating condition would allow.

During the three and a half years Rob lived with Hodgkin's disease, he refused to indulge in self-pity or the chronic complaining that entraps those who are defeated by sickness. When his parents expressed the anger and frustration provoked by their inability to protect Rob, he reminded them of the patients he had met who were "far worse off than he was." Good-natured and humorous, he helped his parents avoid despair. When they questioned him about his apparent daydreaming, Rob admitted that he was praying; but he said no more about it than that.

Rob's father Morgan says of his son, "Rob's faith was strong though inward, not worn on his sleeve. He accepted the ordeal God asked him to endure." When Loretta decided to take Rob to Lourdes, she was "looking for a miracle, pure and simple." Rob did not encourage his mother in her hope for a cure. He prayed quietly at the Grotto, revealing nothing about his expectations of Mary. Whatever passed between them remained a private affair.

His fellow pilgrims saw in Rob a tall, emaciated young man, his face hollowed out by illness, his blue eyes remarkably recessed in dark circles etched by suffering. Some could not look at him without glancing away. Sensing his fragility, they were offended that death should make its presence felt in a place so permeated with hope for healing.

In the course of the pilgrimage, Loretta, realizing that there was nothing more she could do for Rob, turned him over to Mary. She let go of the son she had been clinging to with such possessive desperation. "For a reason I can't explain, I prayed for God's will to be done and for Mary to give me strength for whatever I had to face," she recalls.

After his return from Lourdes, Rob declined visibly each day. His legs were swollen and he alternated between painful consciousness and the respite of sleep. For the first time, his equanimity in suffering temporarily deserted him. Rob told his parents that had he not been a Catholic, he would have overdosed on drugs. They were devastated by the knowledge that their son, so courageous and gentle throughout his illness, should be allowed to feel such futility. "Those were the days I felt Our Lady had let us down," Loretta says.

Rob died a month after his Lourdes pilgrimage. His family was torn between gratitude that his suffering had ended and resentment that he had not been cured. Gradually, they learned to accept the empty place in their home.

Morgan says he accepted the loss of his son grudgingly because he hadn't the wisdom to understand why God called Rob so soon. Loretta's friends see in her the inner strength gained by resigning her will to the will of the Father.

Both parents are convinced that Mary has guided their son into eternity. They feel blessed by the richness of Rob's presence with them for 20 years. And they are secure in knowing that his Mother will never allow the least suffering to touch him again.

# Prayer

Acknowledging your unity with all who mourn, with all who suffer the empty place at the family table, with all who respect God's right to call each of us according to his plan, turn to Mary in prayer:

*Be there, Mother,*
*when pain threatens*
*to cast me adrift*
*in hopelessness.*

*Be there*
*when loss summons me*
*to the brow*
*of despair.*

*Be there*
*when I, like Christ,*
*am lifted up*
*to the Father.*

*"And from my flesh I shall see God;*
*my inmost being is consumed with longing."*
*(Job 19:26)*

*Lord, that I may have life everlasting!*

# *Response*

Console someone who is in mourning or someone who cannot accept a personal loss. Listen attentively as they express their grief or resentment. Encourage and support them in whatever way is most natural to you. If appropriate, suggest that they entrust themselves to Mary.

Read and reflect on Mark 14:32-39, The Agony in the Garden. Hear Christ pouring out his heart to his Father. Extend your reflection into a meditative praying of the first sorrowful mystery of the rosary.

Examine your own convictions about everlasting life by reading what St. Paul has to say about faith and the Resurrection (1 Corinthians 15:12-19). Discuss this passage with a friend, exploring whether your own words and actions at the time of someone's death clearly reflect your Christian faith.

# Heal Me, Lord

## *Meditation*

We have come to the final day of pilgrimage. Whether you yet know it or not, Mary has heard your prayer and has begun her healing work. What she began at Cana, she continues today. Mary must care for us. It is both her nature and her God-directed vocation to do so.

But do we believe? Do we allow Mary to mother us? Or do we demand the proof of sudden miracles? Perhaps, for some of us, even that would not be enough. Resolve to pray for the faith that moves mountains—and the faith that endures when those mountains still stand.

Take a candle with you and proceed down the path which has become so familiar to you. The path is your pilgrim's way, a sign of commitment to seeking Mary. Recognize that you will always be a pilgrim, always moving forward in faith, until the day when your Mother leads you into eternal light. Let your heart be moved by anticipation. Say with the psalmist:

> *As the hind longs for the running waters,*
> *so my soul longs for you, O God.*
> *(Psalm 42:2)*

Enjoy the music of the stream, hearing it as the welcome voice of a friend. The water is awash in sunlight, evoking a pristine time when the world was new. When you reach the cavern, your horizon opens up to encompass each place of pilgrimage you have visited in the past seven days. Below, across the stream, the field of wild flowers creates a vibrant, moving tapestry. On your side of the stream, the hardwood grove offers its green haven bright with bird-song. Above, the Shrine of the Crowned Woman is clearly visible, and beyond it, in the distance, the hillside bearing the cross.

Sit by the cavern and let each familiar voice penetrate you. The stream speaks to you of penitence and purity, the waters of Baptism, the desire to be cleansed of falsity and sin, the need to be spiritually renewed. Learn innocence from the stream.

The cavern, carved in stone, speaks to you of simplicity and strength. It recalls those hidden places where men and women of God have gone apart to fast and pray like Christ in the desert. From the stone, learn faith, a faith that survives storms and changing times.

Light your candle, placing it in the mouth of the cavern. The candle speaks to you of prayer, prayer that parts the darkness of fear, pain and insecurity. It reminds you of the need to be watchful, awake and vigilant like those five wise maidens who kept their lamps burning until the bridegroom arrived (see Matthew 25:1-13). Learn devotion from the candle.

The field of wild flowers with uplifted faces speaks

to you of the plenitude of God's creative love, of his care profusely bestowed, of his modest desire that you love him in return. Recall that each flower worships him by being the flower he desires it to be, by bending to his breeze rather than standing stiffly in its own way. From the flowers, learn humility.

Hear the sparrows' sweet, sharp notes winging above the rustling leaves. In that simple song, hear the voice of trust, of freedom from worry about what shall be eaten and what shall be worn, of gratitude for all that has been given. From the sparrow, learn praise.

Gaze out across the square and see the faces of your fellow pilgrims. They bear their handicaps with willing acceptance, believing in Jesus' promise: "By patient endurance, you will save your lives" (Luke 21:19). Their eyes, as one, are turned to the woman crowned with stars, the woman they call Mother. From your fellow pilgrims, learn hope.

Now consider that distant cross. It speaks to you of self-denial and sacrifice, of giving all and gaining all. From the Tree of Life, learn that you, who have been loved unto death, must be willing to do likewise.

# Reflection

Somewhere, nearby, Mary is waiting for you. Go to her. Sit at her feet and listen in silence.

She is pleased with your pilgrimage and your confidence in her. The greater your expectations of her, the deeper your trust, the more surely will she act. She understands your need for healing and asks only that you remain open to whatever way her Son chooses to respond. He who turned water into wine can transform your suffering into gladness. He is free to heal by lifting up or bringing low, by cradling or crushing.

Mary looks at you lovingly, taking in every aspect of that self which you are only beginning to uncover. In her face, you see the virtues you must emulate: compassion, prayerfulness, mercy, fidelity, humility, hopefulness.

Aware of your desire to be whole, to experience the deep and constant presence of Christ, to be healed and to be healing, Mary gives you her maternal advice: "Do whatever he tells you" (John 2:5). Let her words echo in your heart.

After you have absorbed Mary's message, go down to the stream. Find the quiet pool you studied on the first day of pilgrimage. Look again at your image. See the beauty Mary sees in you, the reflections of her Son which are visible in this particular way only in you. Observe your handicap in the light of your new awareness. Love the person you see, the God-fathered, Jesus-loved, Mary-mothered person you are.

With peace flowing like a stream inside you, leave the pool and return to the path. Move slowly, preserving the stillness of this place. Keep the memory of Mary before you like a treasured cameo. Praise her with the Hail Mary.

# Profile

U nless you change and become like little children, you will never enter the kingdom of God" (Matthew 18:3). By walking in faith, by proclaiming their need for healing, by petitioning their Mother, pilgrims make themselves spiritual children who recognize their total dependence. They learn to be still and let God be God. They learn to listen to the voices of their brothers and sisters in Christ.

Consider Ray S., 30-year-old father of two sons. The elder, Michael, was born with rubella damage which manifested itself in near blindness, twisted feet, a heart murmur and learning difficulties. After eye surgery, he could distinguish only large objects at close range. His parents feared the consequences of Michael's constant falling and bumping into furniture. When he was two, they decided to take him to Lourdes.

Ray did not consider himself a religious person. "I had problems with the Church and did not attend Mass regularly," he says, adding, "I certainly wasn't in the habit of asking Mary for help." He had simply reached the point he could think of nothing else to do. At the shrine, Ray began pleading for a miracle, an instant cure of Michael's blindness.

After a few days, without his quite realizing how it

happened, Ray found himself spending less time on his knees at the Grotto and more time pushing wheelchairs up the steep streets of Lourdes. "I stopped being selfish about Michael and started helping handicapped pilgrims who needed me. I no longer demanded a miracle," he recalls.

On the eighth day of the pilgrimage, Michael's sight was unchanged. But the child's obvious happiness in "talking to Jesus" at the shrine consoled his parents. They were able to see Michael as a blessing, a special child who would teach his family the meaning of pure faith. Ray volunteered to join the next pilgrimage as a helper of the handicapped. He perseveres in that ministry and organizes fund-raisers for children who want to go to Lourdes.

Michael, who has had additional surgery, is now in a class for children with special needs. He can discern colors and objects that are 10 feet away. He no longer falls and bumps into things. His disposition is invariably pleasant and Ray says that in school, "He always makes sure that the other children receive a share of whatever he gets." Although Michael is smaller than his younger brother Danny, he expresses no jealousy or resentment of him.

One of Michael's favorite pastimes is to lie on the floor by the window where the sun warms the carpet. There he sings original songs to God, melodies his parents describe as love songs expressing Michael's desire to "go to see God at his house."

Because Michael's extensive progress has surprised his doctors and teachers, Ray attributes that progress to Mary's intercession. Lourdes was a turning point for his son and for him. "You learn to quit asking for yourself. My whole life has changed since I decided to trust the Lord to take care of us—and to give Michael a little extra attention," Ray says. That firm trust is supported by the sacramental life to which Ray has returned with an unfamiliar eagerness. The Eucharist enables him to be Christ to the other.

# Prayer

With love for Michael and Ray, and for all those whom you recognize as fellow pilgrims, turn to Mary in prayer:

*Mother, will I remember that faith requires me*
*to forsake the pretense of self-sufficiency*
*and remove the prickly garment of impatience?*

*Will I embrace the human heritage*
*of insecurity and unanswered questions,*
*of waiting*
*like a well-disposed child*
*for the Father's word?*

*Shall I bruise my knees with pleading*
*and turn my back on the one who cannot kneel?*

*No, not if you are with me,*
*not if you refuse to let me go,*
*not if you require of me*
*faith*
*that does justice to its name. Amen.*

*Lord, I believe. Help my unbelief.*

# Response

Make a list of the qualities you admire in Mary. Then, taking an honest look at yourself, write your name next to those qualities which you possess to some degree. Finally, select one virtue which is most important to you. Identify three ways to nurture the desired virtue and begin to work on the first one today.

Remembering Michael, who loves to lie in the sun and sing extemporaneous songs to the Lord, think of the most enjoyable way you have found to get in touch with God. Recreate that experience as soon as possible.

Read and reflect on John 20:11-18. Mary Magdalene at the Tomb. Hear Jesus pronounce your name. Identify with Mary whose hopelessness is changed into ecstatic joy at a single word from Jesus. Let the Scripture prepare you for a meditative praying of the first glorious mystery, the Resurrection. Resolve that your life will proclaim Mary's message: "I have seen the Lord!" (John 20:18)

# A Celebration
for Pilgrims

Y ou have completed your
eight-day pilgrimage. And in seeking Mary, you
have found her Son. There is cause for rejoicing
here, for celebrating your progress in inner healing,
for singing the praises of the Lord.

Together with a friend or several friends use the
following prayer service to celebrate whatever Mary
has done for you during your pilgrimage — or
whatever you, in faith, expect her to do in the days
to come. You may want to substitute prayers,
readings and songs of your own choice.

To complete the celebration, share

refreshments or a festive meal. Even better, let the prayer service be a prelude to a home celebration of the Eucharist.

In preparation, cover a table with an attractive fabric and enthrone your Bible, propping it against a small stand or a few books. Place a large candle next to it. Open the Bible to the first reading, Psalm 103.

Gather symbolic items from your pilgrimage experience: a wooden cross, wild flowers and branches of green leaves, a mirror for the reflecting pool, an old nest or a picture of a songbird. Arrange these on the table.

# *Prayer Service*

Opening Song:    "Gentle Woman" (Rev. Carey
Landry, North American
Liturgy Resources) or
"Immaculate Mary" (the
Lourdes pilgrims' song).

First Reading:    Psalm 103, Praise of Divine
Goodness. (The psalm may be
read together or antiphonally,
using the first line as a response
to each stanza. The reading
might be followed by Psalm
103's musical interpretation:
"Bless the Lord" from *Godspell.*

*Reflect in silence.*

Second Reading:    John 9:1-7, The Man Born Blind.

*Reflect in silence, then share
whatever insights you have on the
reading.*

Leader:    Let us call to mind each person
we know who is in need of
healing.

*Allow time for the group to offer
prayers for people they know.*

Remember, too, our fellow
pilgrims: Joe, Julie and Doris,
Debbie, Oscar and Dolores,
Jackie, Mary, Loretta and
Morgan, Michael and Ray.

Uniting ourselves with them,
may we realize that suffering and
pain can be positive forces when,
through prayer, they lead us on
to compassion and hope. May we
believe, as Thomas Merton said,
that "we are made saints not by
undergoing pain, but by
overcoming it."

Together let us cry out: Lord, we
believe in you.

Response:  Lord, we believe in you.

Leader:  Lord, your friends are sick.
*(Response)*

Say but the word and we shall be
healed. *(Response)*
Lord, make us see. *(Response)*
Lord, make us hear. *(Response)*
Heal us, Lord. *(Response)*
Heal all who call on you in faith.
*(Response)*

Mary, Mother of Jesus and our
Mother,

98

Response:    Pray for us.

*Sing or listen to a favorite hymn,*
*song or reflective instrumental.*

Leader:    Let us address our Mother in the
words of the prayer T.S. Eliot
wove into his poem, "Ash
Wednesday":

Blessèd sister, holy mother, spirit
   of the fountain, spirit of the
   garden,
Suffer us not to mock ourselves
   with falsehood.
Teach us to care and not to care.
Teach us to sit still
Even among these rocks,
Our peace in His will
And even among these rocks
Sister, mother
And spirit of the river, spirit of
   the sea,
Suffer me not to be separated

And let my cry come unto Thee.

Leader:    The pilgrimage is over. The
pilgrimage has just begun.
Through Mary to Jesus. Amen.

Response:    Amen.

# *Postscript*

Julie died of cancer on June 17, 1980, at the age of six. In the funeral homily, her close friend and pastor called her "a living reminder of our destiny." He compared her to the little lamb the Eastern shepherd uses when he wants to move his flock to a new pasture. "He picks up the lamb and sets it on a hill. When the other sheep see the lamb, they follow it there. Even now we are heading that way."

Sweet Julie, little lamb of Jesus, may St. Bernadette the shepherdess be always your companion, Our Lady of Lourdes your maternal guide, and Jesus your best, best friend.